Billy Graham Talks to Teenagers

BILLY GRAHAM

MARSHALL, MORGAN & SCOTT
London

MARSHALL, MORGAN & SCOTT LTD.
BLUNDELL HOUSE
GOODWOOD ROAD
LONDON S.E.14

First Edition 1960
Seventh Impression 1968
"Star" edition 1971

ISBN 0 551 05058 6

Made and Printed by Cahill and Co, Dublin and London

CONTENTS

PREFACE

Billy Graham has a heart for teenagers. He began his evangelistic ministry as a staff evangelist for Youth for Christ International back in 1945, and today in his great city-wide crusades sets aside a "Youth Night" each week.

Youth for Christ Magazine has been privileged to print a number of articles by Billy Graham, and we have gathered some of them into this one attractive book. The three messages "When Christ Was a Teenager," "God's Juvenile Delinquent," and "Let's Kill the Giants" were given at the 1958 San Francisco Crusade and are included here in digest form with Billy Graham's kind permission.

These articles and messages are filled with God's Word and seek to glorify Jesus Christ. I know that multiplied thousands of young people will be challenged and helped by this book.

TED W. ENGSTROM

"I WAS 16 . . . AND LOVED BASEBALL!"

Billy Graham's Personal Testimony

I'll never forget my first year in high school. Babe Ruth, the great "King of Swat," came to my home town of Charlotte, N. C., to play an exhibition game. All of us kids were on the front seats shouting and yelling at the top of our lungs. My father, who had taken us to the game, arranged for me to shake hands with the great Babe. I will never forget the thrill of shaking hands with the fellow who was the idol of all our young hearts. I didn't wash my hands for about three days. The next day at school I was the envy of all my friends.

During my last years in high school my keenest ambition was to be a professional baseball player. I dreamed of playing in Wrigley Field in Chicago, Yankee Stadium, etc. I "ate" up the sports pages.

When I was 16, after finishing a game, I was invited to a church. I was told that a "fighting preacher" was to preach. I was interested, for anything about a scrap or a fight was all I wanted. I forsook my studies and went to church. To my amazement, it was a great evangelistic campaign and 5,000 people were gathered.

I sat in the rear of the building, curiously watching all the strange happenings. I wasn't quite sure what would take place next. I had always thought of religion as more or less "sissy stuff," and that a fellow who was going to be an athlete would have no time for such things. It was all right for old men and girls, but not for real "he-men" with red blood in their veins. I had gone to church some, but that was all.

A great giant of a man stood and began to preach in such a way as I had never heard a man preach. Halfway through his message he pointed right in my direction and said,

"Young man, you are a sinner."

I thought he was talking to me, so I ducked behind the person in front of me and hid my face! The idea of his calling me a sinner!

"Why, I'm as good as anybody," I told myself. "I live a good, clean, healthy, moral life. I'm even a member of a church, though I seldom go."

But then he began to quote Scripture. "All have sinned and come short of the glory of God." "There is none righteous, no not one," and others. For the first time in my life I realised that I was a sinner, that my soul was bound for hell and that I needed a Saviour.

But when he gave the invitation, I rushed out into the night and made my way home.

I'll never forget the struggle that followed. All night long I wrestled and fought. The next day I could hardly wait for evening, so I could get back to the service. This night I sat near the front. When the preacher got up this time, he seemed to smile at me. He said in tenderest tones that "God commendeth his love towards us in that while we were yet sinners Christ died for us."

I thought, "This is for me! I'm a sinner. God loves me."

When the invitation was given, I made my way to the front with the others. I gave my hand to the preacher (Mordecai Ham) and my heart to the Saviour. Immediately joy, peace and assurance flooded my soul. My sins, which were many, were gone! For the first time I had met the Person who became the Hero of my life.

I had sought thrills! I found them in Christ. I had looked for something that would bring perfect joy and happiness! I found it in Christ. I had looked for something that would bring pleasure and that would satisfy the deepest longing of my heart! I found it in Christ. "In thy presence is fullness of joy; at thy right hand are pleasures for evermore."

Christ is the Hero and Idol of my heart. He challenges, thrills and satisfies.

IF I WERE 17 TODAY

As told to Mel Larson

QUESTION: *Would you, today, make the same decision to accept Christ as you did when you were a teenager?*

ANSWER: Yes, I most certainly would. Ecclesiastes 12:1 says "Remember now thy Creator in the days of thy youth, while the evil days come not, nor the years draw nigh, when thou shalt say, I have no pleasure in them." By making my decision for Christ in high school I avoided a lot of trouble that fellows and girls face in college, as I now had Christ within me.

QUESTION: *How would you witness for Christ in high school?*

ANSWER: The main thing in witnessing and soul-winning is to live such a victorious life in Christ that people will be drawn to Him through you, just like a magnet. If a student needs help in one way or another, you should be there to assist in any way possible. Take this for an example. Say you go to a party and you see a fellow or girl having a hard time getting acquainted, or who obviously is lonely. Right there is where you can make yourself friendly to that person. In so doing, that person will be interested in what made you concerned about him.

I would seek in some way or another to witness to every one in my class. Remember, it's the way you live that often means a great deal more than what you say.

QUESTION: *How would you go about reading your Bible?*

ANSWER: One main word on that: *systematically.* I would read some in the Old Testament. I would buy myself a modern translation, such as Phillips, which is good for young people.

QUESTION: *What about church and young people's society?*

ANSWER: I would attend as faithfully and regularly as I possibly could. Right there is where you indicate your real witness for Christ. Don't criticise your church or your pastor. Your church is just what you put into it.

QUESTION: *How about prayer habits and schedules?*

ANSWER: Don't pray only when you feel like it, or you'll never pray. The disciples asked Jesus if He would teach them to pray. We also need to be taught to pray. Prayer is often a matter of practice and you learn best by praying, not by reading books on prayer. Schedule your prayer pattern around your daily life and habits.

QUESTION: *How would you decide on a college?*

ANSWER: This is always a difficult decision to make. Some people feel we should go to a secular college in order to witness more for our Lord. In many cases, however, young people need rooting and grounding in the doctrines of Christianity and a Christian school is tops along this line. I would seek to attend an accredited school if at all possible. Talk much to your parents, to trusted counsellors and to teachers and professors about the school you should attend.

QUESTION: *How would you regard sports and other extracurricular activities?*

ANSWER: I would get into as many as possible, but with moderation. They do you a great deal of good and you learn much from them. But, don't overdo in high school. I did in baseball when I was in high school and my grades suffered because of it.

QUESTION: *What would your attitude be towards studies and class assignments?*

ANSWER: I would take the subjects I liked the least and study them the most. For one thing, this is an excellent method of discipline. Also, try always to be learning something new. Do things you do not like to do and you'll be amazed at what you accomplish. That includes those subjects you shy away from all the time.

A key lesson we need to learn in high school is to discipline ourselves. It takes something, believe me, to walk over and turn off that TV set and go and read the Bible or

8

do your homework. It's hard for me to see how you can study with the TV set or radio going.

QUESTION: *What about girls, dates and going steady?*

ANSWER: I definitely would not go steady. I don't think most fellows or girls are mature enough to go steady. Be friends with all of them. You'll find you'll be much happier and avoid some heartache.

QUESTION: *Hot rodding and cars in general are teenager passions. How would you rate them?*

ANSWER: Go easy on cars. I say that carefully and yet forcefully. Look at it this way. It's not really much of a witness for Christ to go around endangering the lives of others, is it?

QUESTION: *How would you regard the advice of your parents? Is it up to date?*

ANSWER: Listen to them! You think they are "old fogies" now, but when you get to be 25 you'll see they weren't so bad. When you get to be 35 you'll wonder at how much they really knew and how little you knew.

QUESTION: *You didn't have TV when you were young. How would you handle it now?*

ANSWER: As I mentioned under studies, it takes a disciplined mind to turn off TV and go and study or read your Bible. Whenever I am home for any period of time I find it too easy to sit and sit in front of the television set. There is of course much good on TV, but be careful that it doesn't take too much of your precious time when you should be studying or witnessing for Christ.

QUESTION: *You had other types of music to face when you were young, but how would you regard Rock 'n' Roll?*

ANSWER: I rarely hear any of it, but I do feel that it has gotten out of hand. Anything that whips young people into a frenzy is bad, it seems to me. I often have been disturbed by what has happened to teenagers after they listen to it. If I were 17 today I'd stay as far away from it as I could.

QUESTION: *One final question: Would you feel*

discouraged about life if you were 17 *today? Is there hope for today's teenagers?*

ANSWER: The world situation often looks dark, but we have Christ and He is all we need. If I were 17 today I would make definite plans for my future. I would go to college. A college education is more essential today than it has ever been. I would get as much Bible training as I possibly could, no matter for what field I was headed. I have never regretted the training I have had.

Words which Abraham Lincoln once said come to me often when I think of young people and their future. He stated on one occasion, "I will prepare myself, and some day my chance will come."

With Christ in your heart and at your side, give life everything you've got.

DIG INTO YOUR BIBLE, TEENAGER !

" Billy, I just don't have time to read and study the Bible as I should. There is so much to do, so many things demanding care and attention that the time just isn't there."

I've had that thought tossed at me by young people in many parts of the world. I always tell them,

"Unless you are reading and studying your Bible systematically, your efforts for Christ are being robbed of much of their effectiveness."

They often have replied,

"Well, what suggestions would you have for us along Bible study lines?"

Here are a few of them. May they be used by God to challenge you to dig into your Bible.

1. GET YOURSELF A GOOD STUDY BIBLE. It is well to have a Bible to carry with you to school and to church, but I would suggest that you also have a larger study Bible which you can keep in your room or on your desk for studying and reading. Ask your pastor or check your nearest book store on such a Bible. Along with Old and

New Testaments they usually carry much other material of study help.

2. KEEP A NOTEBOOK ALONGSIDE WHEN YOU READ. Jot down thoughts and reactions which come from certain verses or portions. There are many systems of Bible study available, all of which are excellent, but do not be afraid to write down your own thoughts as you read and meditate. These can well represent God speaking to you through His Word.

3. LEARN TO USE A CONCORDANCE. Your study Bible likely will have one in the back of the book. Many other concordances are available, all of which are excellent. *Crudens* is one of them. These books are invaluable in helping you find verses which have the same word. Also, you may remember part of a verse but not know where to locate it; the concordance is your solution there.

4. GET A NAVE'S TOPICAL BIBLE. Outside of the Bible, this is the book I depend on more than any other. I have bought scores of copies and have given them to many outstanding leaders. They have all testified that it has helped to change their ministry. There is no book that has helped me more in my study than Nave's Topical Bible. I have recommended it publicly in all campaigns and use it daily in my study and nightly from the platform.

It is a large, heavy book of some 1,600 pages, including the index. It is a digest of the Holy Scriptures under 20,000 topics and sub-topics, with 100,000 references to the Scriptures. Orville J. Nave is the author and it was first copyrighted in 1896. The object of this book is to bring together in cyclopaedic form and under familiar headings all that the Bible teaches on particular subjects.

5. CHECK OTHER VERSIONS. Do not be afraid to look into other translations other than the King James. There are many excellent ones published and I will not list any for fear of missing some. These versions give you different slants on certain key verses you may be using in developing a talk for your youth society or Bible Club. Checking these may well involve additional time and effort, but you will be richly rewarded time and time again by the jewels uncovered in such digging.

6. PAUSE TO PRAY AS YOU STUDY. If God shows you something in His Word that thrills you, stop right there and thank Him for it. If things are going a bit rough as you study, ask Him for divine guidance and help. Prayer is a vital part of Bible study and meditation.

7. MEMORISE AS MUCH AS YOU CAN. I do not hesitate at all to recommend the Navigator system. We use it in our follow-up work with our converts and it is excellent. Take a key verse or two from your morning quiet time and commit it to memory during the day. Jot it down on a piece of paper for reference during the hours at school or at work. Hide God's Word in your heart. It will enrich you greatly.

8. TAKE TIME TO READ THE BIBLE. Not studying it, but merely reading it. Get into an easy chair and spend an hour or so reading it. Go through entire books at one sitting. Concentrate as you read and after such a period you will be surprised at how refreshed you feel.

9. CARRY YOUR BIBLE WITH YOU AS MUCH AS POSSIBLE. This includes to school, to work, and to church. It is a testimony to the world and also is readily available for the opportunities which come your way in telling people about Christ. Remember again, it is not what you say that counts, but what the Bible says.

CLOSING THOUGHTS. Read as long a portion in your daily devotions as fits your personal situation. The length depends largely on you as an individual. Never allow your family devotions to take the place of your quiet time. Do not be afraid, as you study, to list questions that come to your mind. Go to your pastor with them. He will be happy to answer them for you.

If you find your mind wandering as you study, quit until you can concentrate. Do not wander through a chapter or two, get nothing out of it, then go on your way feeling that you have completed your studying for that day. Better to read one verse knowingly than one chapter and not know what was in it.

May I repeat again to each one of you, *dig into your Bible!* It is rich. It is boundless in its blessing. You will never be able to reach its greatest depths. It is as important to your spiritual life as food is to your physical and mental existence.

And the service for Christ that will count will have a direct relationship to the amount of time you spend in its sacred pages.

Go to it!

TO BRIDES AND GROOMS

(*And All Hoping to Be Such*)

"We are gathered together in the sight of God and these witnesses, to join these two in holy matrimony."

God performed the first marriage in the Garden of Eden. He ordained that man and woman should marry. Jesus sanctified marriage when He went to the marriage feast in Cana of Galilee.

Young people, look to your Bible when thinking about any matter, including getting married. Read Ephesians 5:21-31: *"Submitting yourselves one to another in the fear of God. Wives, submit yourselves unto your husbands, as unto the Lord. For the husband is the head of the wife, even as Christ is the head of the church: and He is the Saviour of the body. Therefore as the church is subject unto Christ, so let the wives be to their own husbands in every thing. Husbands, love your wives, even as Christ also loved the church, and gave Himself for it; That He might sanctify and cleanse it with the washing of water by the Word, that He might present it to Himself a glorious church, not having spot or wrinkle, or any such thing; but that it should be holy and without blemish. So ought men to love their wives as their own bodies. He that loveth his wife loveth himself. For no man ever yet hated his own flesh; but nourisheth and cherisheth it, even as the Lord the church: For we are members of His body, of His flesh, and of His bones. For this cause shall a man leave his father and mother, and shall be joined unto his wife, and they shall be one flesh."*

13

Marriage has been ordained by God, and God has sanctified marriage by putting a great deal concerning it in the Word of God. However, in America we have left God's rules out, by and large, and as a result, 25 per cent of those that come to the marriage altar end up in a divorce court. We are told that 50 per cent of all marriages in the United States are unhappy marriages and that only 25 per cent of marriages are actually supremely happy ones.

One of our greatest needs in America today is for instruction to those who are getting married, concerning the things of God and God's rules concerning marriage.

The following prescription I believe will be a guarantee to a happy marriage.

First, let me suggest to you that are contemplating marriage that you be sure that both of you know Christ as your Saviour. That is very essential, because most of the unhappy marriages in America today are those that are outside the Christian fold. Be sure that he or she is a Christian. Many people do not know what it means to be a Christian. They think that a Christian is a person who lives a good, decent, moral life. Some think a Christian is a person who treats his neighbour as himself. That is part of the Christian life, but that is not essentially Christian. A Christian is a person who, recognising that he is a sinner, has come to Jesus by faith and has accepted Him as Lord and Saviour. Has that young man—that young woman—you are thinking about marrying become a Christian? Are you sure?

Secondly, be sure that the young man or young woman is a yielded Christian. There is a difference between a Christian and a yielded Christian. A yielded Christian is one that has turned over every area of his life and personality to the Lord Jesus Christ. He has been filled with the Spirit of God. He or she is producing the fruit of the Spirit: love, joy, peace, long-suffering, gentleness—all of the fruits of the Spirit which are very essential to a happy home.

Thirdly, it is important to be sure that you marry *God's choice*. God has a plan for our lives. He has a plan for your life. He has it all blueprinted and has the ideal

14

choice for you. He has somebody already picked out for you. Be sure that the one you are joining hands with in holy matrimony is God's choice for you.

Fourthly, it is important that you love one another. Love is very essential to a happy marriage. Now, physical attraction is only temporary. So many today are joining hands because they are attracted to one another physically. That is no basis for a happy and successful marriage. True love is based on mutual understanding, congeniality and spiritual affinity. Be sure that you have proper love, because love is based also on respect and admiration. If you respect him and admire him, that is a basis for true love. And also remember that love grows! After you have been married ten years you will love him or her far more than the day you walked to the altar, if it's true love.

Fifthly, you must obey certain rules for a Christian marriage. I would like to suggest that you establish a family altar. By that I mean that you have daily prayer and Bible reading in your home. That should actually start before the marriage. If you cannot pray with your husband-to-be or your wife-to-be now, it's very doubtful that you can pray after marriage. So start praying together and studying and reading the Bible together every time you go out on a date, every time you get together. Start the home right.

Sixthly, there is a God-given place in the home for each of you. The wife is to submit herself to the husband, to obey the husband. That word " obey " is old-fashioned, but it's in the Bible and God says it is essential to a happy and successful marriage.

This closing thought. Husbands, you are to love and honour your wives. Treat them as sweethearts all the days of your life and your love will grow as the years go by.

You also must pray and seek God's will about children. There is nothing that will join you together like children.

You must be faithful in the church. Let your social life revolve around the life in your church. Every time the church doors are open, you be there, you and your entire family, faithful in church.

Keep these things in mind and I am convinced that you can have a happy and successful marriage. It is my prayer, and the prayer of every pastor and minister, that you will have a happy and successful marriage as you give your lives completely to Christ and as you obey these precepts, commandments, thoughts and suggestions. They are essential to a happy and successful marriage.

BILLY GRAHAM, SPORTS WRITER

Reprinted through courtesy of
The Nashville Tennessean
and sports editor Raymond Johnson

Ever since I was knee high to a duck I've loved sports. I've played baseball, football, basketball, tennis, golf and about everything else that comes under the category of sports. I am a good baseball fan and a terrible golfer.

A great many people have had the mistaken idea that a real Christian should not be interested in athletics and sports. I believe that one of the greatest ways to combat the social evil of juvenile delinquency is to put more emphasis on sports. I have been happy to learn all that Raymond Johnson and THE TENNESSEAN have been doing to promote sports in Nashville. I think it's a good thing!

A real Christian is a good sportsman. Although all Christians are not superb athletes, it can be said that all true followers of Christ have the spirit of fair play. That is why so many outstanding athletes are Christians. Gil Dodds, the "Flying Parson"; Donn Moomaw, UCLA's famous All-American; Herb Dudley, Clearwater's great softball pitcher who got 55 strike-outs in one game, and Bob Mathias, the decathlon king of the Olympics, are all fine Christians with lots of drive, power and polish. They excel on the track, the gridiron and the diamond because they not only have a strong competitive spirit, perfect coordination and better-than-average ability, but because they have strong, courageous, fighting hearts which give them an edge over their opposition.

There is a verse in the Bible obviously drawn from the athletic contest of that ancient day. It reads: "Wherefore seeing we also are compassed about with so great a cloud of witnesses, let us lay aside every weight, and sin which doth so easily beset us, and let us run with patience the race that is set before us" (Hebrews 12:1). In this verse the Christian life is compared to a great track meet. The stadiums are packed to capacity, the contestants are relieved of the great weights which they have strapped to their legs during their training period, they run patiently and untiringly towards the goal; and victory goes to the strongest and swiftest.

Three training essentials for athletics are suggested by this text of Scripture. The first is: *cleanliness*. "Let us lay aside every sin." Every coach knows that clean living is one of the bases of physical power. You simply cannot abuse your body, be addicted to filthy habits, and be a star on the athletic field. I know many young men who showed promise of being outstanding in their chosen sport; but success went to their heads — they began to drink, gamble and run around. It wasn't long until sin took its toll and they were at the bottom of the heap — just another "has-been."

Years ago men thought that if a fellow didn't drink and run with the fast set he wasn't a real he-man. Now we are discovering that drinking and other forms of body-wrecking pleasures are signs of weakness rather than manliness. It takes a better man to live a clean life — free from the stimulants, depressants and drugs — than to be artificially "hopped up." To be a good athlete is similar to being a good Christian. You must lay aside every sin. You say, "That's pretty rough." But, believe me, it pays off every time. It pays off in more strength, more drive, more skill, more friends and more victories.

The second thing suggested by the verse I mentioned is *concentration*. "Let us run the race that is set before us." Life is a challenge. In every field of endeavour there is plenty of room at the top. The world is crying for leaders, but only those who set for themselves lofty and noble goals will be the leaders of tomorrow. Concentration always pays off. The fellow who has a general interest in everything usually isn't too good at anything. Jack-of-all-trades is usually master of none.

Look at Ben Hogan, the master of golf. Ben lives golf, sleeps golf, eats golf and dreams golf. I heard him on television the other night say that 70 per cent of golf was thinking through every shot. It takes concentration. While many of the other golfers are out on the town at night, Ben is in his room chipping balls with his niblick. He has one goal. Flawless golf and concentration are the secrets of his success. I was at St. Andrews in Scotland some time ago and they were telling me how he won the British Open. They said he practised more than any man that had ever been at St. Andrews, that he drove himself to concentrated practice.

In character building and in living the Christian life concentration is important also. Paul, the great apostle, underlined this fact when he said: "This one thing I do . . . I press towards the mark for the prize of the high calling of God in Christ Jesus." Paul had set for himself a high goal. He concentrated all of his talents, thought and energy in an all-out effort to attain that goal. As we know, he achieved that goal and has gone down in history as chief of saints.

The last thought suggested in our verse from Hebrews is *consecration*. This means to be "completely given over to" — or as we would say, "completely sold on." For a man to be a good baseball player he must be completely sold on the game. For a man to be a good golfer or tennis player he must be completely sold on these particular games.

If an athlete lets money, pride, bad habits take precedence over the development of his skill and ability in his sport, he will never reach the top. I have known quite a few fellows who have won lots of trophies but eventually lost out in the biggest struggle of all — the moral battle. That is a mighty sad thing for our athletic contest, a symbol on the physical level of the bigger fight on the spiritual and moral levels. Some of you fellows have heard your team members say, "Come on now, fellows, we've got to win. This is the big one!"

Well, I've known the thrill of winning a tough ball game and of winning a golf match on the last hole. That's a lot of fun. But to me the biggest thrill is to win the big one—the spiritual battle of life. We can't do that alone. We are going to need help. Some team work is needed. In fact, we are going to have to call on the Master Coach, Jesus Christ.

If you will read the second verse of the 12th chapter of Hebrews, it says: "Looking unto Jesus, the Author and Finisher of our Faith." There is the secret of spiritual victory. Just as you respect and need the advice of your coach in order to be a winner in athletics you need the help of Jesus Christ to be a spiritual winner. He is more interested in what you are and who you are, He is more concerned with how you played the game, than whether you won or lost a game or two.

I think that this is what Grantland Rice meant when he closed his poem to champions with these words:

> And when that one Great Scorer comes
> To write against your name,
> He'll write not that you won or lost,
> But how you played the game.

WHEN CHRIST WAS A TEENAGER

Very few of us stop to realise that there was a period in Jesus' life when He was a teenager. The Bible doesn't tell us too much about this period, but it tells us something. It says in Luke 2:51-52 — "And he (Jesus) went down with them (His parents), and came to Nazareth, and was subject unto them . . . And Jesus increased in wisdom and stature, and in favour with God and man."

The world we live in today is a little bit different from the world Jesus lived in. I read in a magazine article that the average teenager costs his parents about $15,000 to get him through that period of life somebody has called "over fool's hill." And the teenager is supposed to drink 4,732 bottles of soft drinks during that period, eat 4,298 bowls of cereal, 2,096 pounds of hamburger, 6,156 cones of ice cream, 5,408 bars of candy, 5,624 eggs, and 5,720 hot dogs! He'll wear $2,160 worth of clothing and 78 pairs of shoes; and he'll buy 170 records. That's what teenagers are made of!

But I also read some disturbing things about teenagers. A survey by one of our leading magazines revealed that less than half of the high school and college graduates in the country could identify the Bill of Rights. Only 35 per cent could give a single advantage of our economic system over Russia's. Only 40 per cent could work a simple equation, and only 25 per cent could give the chemical composition of table salt.

I don't know what a teenager is—but I do know that teenagers in America have some mighty big problems facing them. Young people in America face the greatest problems of any young people in the history of the world. We live constantly in the threat of an atomic war, and in the midst of revolts all over the world. It seems like the Devil has the world like a great big bowl and he's stirring it up with a big stick! And teenagers are caught in the middle of all this. They are maturing faster physically than they are mentally, and they are having to make important decisions. One teenager, when asked what his biggest problem was, replied, "I've got so many problems, I don't know which to put down first!"

Living in this world of gadgets and amusements, with its tremendous emphasis on sex, plenty of leisure time, a lot of money, plus insecurity and sophistication, today's teenagers face real problems. The world today may be different from the world in Jesus' day, but the basic problems of young people are the same. Teenagers today can learn much from Christ as a teenager.

Christ had the right kind of parents, and He respected them. One of the problems young people face today is delinquent parents. God is going to hold parents responsible for a great deal of what is going on among teenagers. I have some suggestions to parents of teenagers. Teenagers need to be treated as adults, they need to be considered. And they need love and encouragement more than criticism. Parents need to set an example for their young people. Young people don't need *things* or more money; they need more love, more attention, more time with their parents.

Then, young people also need discipline — and they *want* to be disciplined. They want to be controlled. They need spiritual guidance, too. "Train up a child in the way he should go; and when he is old, he will not depart from it" says Proverbs 22:6. I've never known a home to break where Christ was the centre, where they had daily Bible reading and prayer in the home. And there may be trouble in your home, teenager, because *you* are not living for Christ. Your parents are Christians, but you have rebelled against them and resented their religion. Give your life to Christ and your home will be what God wants it to be.

The Bible says that *Christ increased in stature,* which indicates physical fitness. American young people are getting mighty soft. A recent study shows that European young people are five times healthier and stronger than American youth! Almost 90 per cent of the American youth failed in physical fitness tests that the Europeans could pass just like that!

We ought to be developing our bodies. The Bible says that our bodies are temples of the Holy Spirit, and that we are to present our *bodies* as living sacrifices to God. Are you living a clean life? Are you doing anything that harms your body, like giving in to sensual passions? You can take that creative energy that we call sex, dedicate it to Jesus Christ, and He will use it to build you into a strong person, physically, mentally, morally, and spiritually, Lose the battle with sex—and you lose the battle of life!

The Scripture says that Christ not only grew in stature, but also in *favour with men.* This is social growth. Jesus had a social life. He wasn't a monk, concealing himself from everyone. No, He was a social person who ate with publicans and sinners and attended weddings and dinners. And He wants you to have a good time socially,

21

too, but in the right way. There is nothing in the Bible that says you must go around with a long face just because you are a Christian. No! You should go around with a smile, having a good time in a clean and wholesome way, with Christ at the centre of your social life. The crowd of young people that knows Jesus Christ is the crowd having the best time in America today.

Christ can come into your life and bring out your true personality and make you winsome. He conquers the fears that retard you socially. He takes away the self-centredness and makes you radiant with a joy that will overflow into the group you mingle with. A true Christian has an inner radiance that is a social asset. I don't believe any girl can be truly beautiful apart from Christ. And, fellows, Jesus Christ can straighten your shoulders and give you a clear eye and a strong face. He can put character into your life! He can make you the complete man that you want to be! Let him take over in your life!

Then, when Christ was a teenager, *He increased in wisdom*. That comes from study, and the Bible says that we are to grow in grace and the knowledge of Jesus Christ. "The fear of the Lord is the beginning of wisdom." God gives wisdom and understanding. When you come to Christ, your mind is involved, because He affects the entire personality. He demands your mind, your intellectual life, so give it to Him. All the wisdom of this world is foolishness to God, and the message of the cross sounds simple-minded to the wise; but to us who are saved, it is the power of God. Learn all that you can, and especially get to know the Bible. It will make a better Christian, a better person out of you.

Most important, it says that *Christ grew in favour with God*. This means that He grew spiritually. He studied the Word of God; he prayed to His Father in heaven; He grew spiritually.

Now, you can't grow spiritually unless you have come to Christ to *receive* eternal life. Has there been a moment in your life when you surrendered to Him? Has Jesus Christ changed you so that you are overcoming temptation and growing in spiritual things? Oh, you've tried to live the Christian life; you've tried to overcome this or that temptation, but you've failed! Why? *Because you are trying to do it in your own strength.* You must first come to Christ and receive Him into your life. When you do, He lives in you and gives you a new dynamic for living. He helps you wherever you are: on the campus, with the old gang, in your home.

Right now, come to Jesus Christ! Admit your failures, then open your heart to Him! He'll make you the kind of Christian teenager you ought to be—and that you really want to be!

GOD'S JUVENILE DELINQUENT

If there was one fellow that God had trouble with, it was Samson. I call him "God's Juvenile Delinquent." Mr. J. Edgar Hoover has said that juvenile crime in America has increased 10 per cent in one year. He's alarmed, and *every* American should be alarmed with him. Forty-one per cent of all arrests for serious crimes in New York last year involved youth under twenty-one. In fact, many of our young people are getting into trouble before they are eight years old! One authority says that fellows and girls are getting into trouble at an earlier age and are committing more vicious crimes than at any other time in history. It is predicted that shortly one boy in five will have a police record by the time he is twenty years old.

Many people are trying to analyse the delinquency problem, but in most cases they are dealing only with symptoms. We hear a great deal about teenage insecurity, bad neighbourhoods, too much leisure time and not enough parental control, suggestive movies and books, television, and so on. These all contribute to the moral deterioration of many young people, but they are, in my opinion, only symptoms. The cause of *all causes* is something else, and I want to show it to you.

Samson was an unusual person, born at a critical time in the history of his country Israel. The Philistines had

23

oppressed Israel for many years, and God gave Samson the greatest opportunity any man could ever want. He was a strong man—we all know that—yet he failed miserably! He had the best heritage, home, and training of almost any man in the Old Testament, yet he missed the boat!

Now, the root of Samson's trouble was not a broken home, or his neighbourhood, or the school he attended. His problem was the problem of millions today, and it may be *your* problem, teenager!

Samson was a strong man, a rugged he-man who was handsome and attracted the girls wherever he went. He was a pretty keen fellow, too, when you consider some of the tricks he pulled. Like catching 300 foxes, tieing their tails together with fire brands between their tails, and sending them out across the fields of the Philistines! When his enemies tried to catch him, he just picked up the gate of the city and took it away! He had beautiful and unusually long hair, and God warned him never to cut it because it was the symbol of his strength and his dedication to God. Samson was young, with all of the enthusiasm and potentials of youth. He had godly parents who sought divine guidance in rearing him. Most of all, God had a plan for his life, a plan that meant conquering the enemy and making Samson a real hero.

Now, Samson had all these advantages, and *you* have advantages, too. Why, you have advantages over other young people and over every other generation that ever lived! You have advantages over other young people in every other country of the world. You have everything to make you the kind of teenager you ought to be, everything to get the most out of life. God has a plan for *your* life just as He had one for Samson, and you can follow it or reject it. Samson had some problems, and because of these problems he missed God's best for his life.

The first problem he had was a *romantic problem*. There comes a time in a boy's life when he becomes aware of the opposite sex, and that happened to Samson. He went down to Timnath and lost his heart to a girl and got his life all mixed up with sex.

There's nothing wrong with sex, and the Bible adopts

24

no "hush-hush" attitude on the subject. But the wrong emphasis on sex has affected almost every phase of life today—movies, plays, books, magazines, advertising. This great creative energy should be dedicated to God, because God will use it and take you to the top. If you don't know Christ, I wouldn't give a snap of my finger for your ability to win this battle with sex. Samson fell in love with a woman in the enemy camp and lost this battle—and kept on losing other battles because he lost this one.

Maybe you have already made some mistakes along this line and committed some sins. God can forgive you! Christ's blood shed on the cross can wash away the foulest sin and make you pure again. But you must come to Christ and let Him forgive you. And Jesus will give you strength when temptations come. In Christ there is power and victory. I don't know of any other power in all the world that can keep you pure and clean and make you what you ought to be, except Jesus Christ.

Samson had another problem—*a parental problem*. A teenager said the other day, "Parents are such a problem!" Samson's parents tried to advise him, but Samson wanted this girl—and he didn't care what it cost him. He didn't care what he did to his parents or how many heartaches he caused. How many young people are filled with selfishness today! All they know is "I, I, I!" Like Samson, they are inconsiderate of their loved ones and determined to have their own way. They want to go their own way, live their own lives, and have no interference or advice from their parents. Yet the Bible says, "Honour thy father and thy mother." It says, "My son, hear the instruction of thy father, and forsake not the law of thy mother." "Children obey your parents in the Lord, for this is right."

Another of Samson's problems—one teenagers face today—was *too much leisure time*. Youthful energy plus too much leisure time equals trouble. Samson began to use his spare time and abounding strength for mischief. Teenagers are filled with restless energy, and this energy has got to be spent somewhere. If you don't get into some constructive activity, you will do like Samson and get into trouble. Teenager, give your life to Christ and then you'll have something to do! You'll have something to challenge you, to take your energy, to build your body, soul, and mind. 'Youth for Christ' is doing a splendid job with high school Bible clubs across the country, with thousands of teenagers gathering every week, some of them top football players and key students in the schools. That's where you can spend your energy and really do some good. Today we need young people who know Christ and live for Him more than we need soldiers or pilots.

But Samson's biggest problem, and your biggest problem, was the *problem of sin*. Samson committed about every sin in the Book! He broke the First Commandment because he didn't put God first in his life. He broke the Second Commandment because he worshipped at the shrine of lust. He didn't honour his parents, and so broke the Fifth Commandment. He broke the Sixth Commandment because he murdered. He broke the Ninth Commandment because he lied, and the Tenth Commandment because he coveted. Samson followed the philosophy of many teenagers today, "Go ahead and live it up! Have a good time!" Yes, Samson did just that, and he reaped corruption and death. Job 4 : 8 says, "Even as I have seen, they that plough iniquity, and sow wickedness, reap the same." Galatians 6:7 warns, "Be not deceived; God is not mocked: for whatsoever a man soweth, that shall he also reap."

God was long-suffering with Samson. God cared for Samson and longed for him to come back for *twenty long years!* God was patient, and God grieved over Samson; and for twenty years Samson was able to "get away" with his sins. Then God said, "I've had enough!" You can "get away" for a year or two, maybe five or even ten, but eventually there will come a time when God will say, "You've gone too far! My patience has run out!" Then you have to pay for your sins, and "The wages of sin is death."

Samson fell in love with a girl named Delilah. The Philistines used Delilah to trick Samson into telling them the secret of his strength. Little by little she enticed Samson until he fell. That's the way sin is: you commit one little

26

sin, and then it leads to bigger sins, and in the end it kills you. Samson told Delilah that his secret was his long hair; and while Samson slept in her lap, she cut off his hair. "The Philistines are upon you!" she cried as the enemy soldiers came out of hiding; and Samson jumped up to fight them, *and he found himself as weak as a fish!* God had left him at the moment when Samson needed Him most!

The Philistines took Samson, burned out his eyes, bound him to the mill wheel in the dungeon, and made him grind all day long. Samson, I want to ask you a question. You sowed your wild oats. You didn't care what people thought, including your father and mother. *Was it worth it all?* You had the greatest potential of any leader in Israel next to Moses, and you failed. You gave way to your sins and passions. *Was it worth it all?* All of us know the answer to that question.

A lot of young people play with sin and think they are going to get away with it. Maybe you have already done some things that you know are wrong. Christ will forgive you! He will change you and give you new power if you will only receive Him! That's what happened to Samson. There in the dungeon, blinded, grinding, bound, Samson said, "God, forgive me! God, forgive me!" Do you know what God did? Oh, the mercy and grace of God! *God forgave Samson.* No matter what we have done, no matter where we have turned, God loves us. Samson turned to God in his hour of need, and God forgave him and gave him back his strength.

"All right, Samson, I'll give you another chance," God said. "But this will be your last victory, and it will cost you your life." Samson got between the pillars of the temple where these heathen were celebrating, and he pulled down the temple! Thousands perished, more than he had ever killed during his life. What a tragic life he had lived because of his sin! Would to God that he had sold out to the Lord!

"Remember now thy creator in the days of thy youth," warns the Bible. Turn to God now, while you're young, and give Christ your life as well as your soul. Talk about

27

good times—why, you don't know what a good time is until you come to Christ! "In thy presence is fullness of joy, at thy right hand there are pleasures for evermore." Don't be one of God's delinquents. Give Christ your *all* while you still have the opportunity, and let Him work out His perfect plan for your life.

LET'S KILL THE GIANTS!

The story of David and the giant Goliath is a familiar one, and probably the favourite story of any dramatic story in the Bible, as far as children are concerned. But it has some lessons in it for young people, too. Because David was just a youth when this event took place.

I want you to get the picture. Israel is facing the Philistines, their enemies. On one side of the valley is the great army of the Philistines, and on the other side is the army of Israel. They have been fighting day in and day out, and one side would win for a while, then the other side. And then suddenly something happens that sends terror into the camp of the Israelites. There comes a man nine feet, four inches tall! That would frighten anyone! He was wearing heavy armour and he was probably the largest man in all recorded history. It was the giant Goliath. And with a voice like a clap of thunder he said to the army of Israel, "Find me a man among Israel who will fight with me. If I win, then the Philistines will win the battle. If I lose, the Philistines will be your servants and Israel will win." This went on for forty days, every morning and every evening. And the Israelites would shudder because there wasn't a man in all Israel who dared to go out and fight.

All the while, David was back home watching his father's sheep. One day his father sent him with ten loaves and three cheeses for his three brothers in the army of Israel. As he approached the army, he heard that monster of a man Goliath say, "I defy the armies of Israel! Give me a man that we may fight together!" David asked, "Who is this man to come down and defy the army of the living God?" And they said, "Well, that's Goliath, the greatest giant in all the world. He can whip twenty men, he's never been defeated in battle—and there's not a man in all Israel who would dare go out in front of him!"

"God will help me defeat him!" David said, and you will remember how he went out with his sling and killed the giant Goliath! What a victory that was—a teenager against a great big giant!

We are facing some giants in the world today—like Communism and the hydrogen bomb, and economic and social tensions around the world. The church, too, faces giants. There is the giant of indifference, for example. And think of the unbelief, the prayerlessness, the hypocrisy that endangers the church, and the fear that keeps many people from taking their stand for Christ.

Young people face giants today. Take bad temper, for example. You've tried to conquer that temper of yours, but you've failed. And there's the giant of jealousy, and that comes from the giant of selfishness. "What can I get out of it?" is your attitude. You don't think of the other person, just yourself. Then there's disobedience—disobeying your parents, your church, and the laws of God. What about laziness, just hanging around doing nothing when the Bible says, "Redeem the time." And sex—what a giant that is! Sex gets out of control and blazes away in your life, and you don't know what to do with it. "I'd give anything if I could control it!" you say.

Vocation is another giant you have to fight: "What shall I do with my life?" There's the great challenge of the mission field today, a challenge that will take red-blooded young men and women who will go all over the world to give the Gospel to the nations. Some of you face the giant of marriage and you don't know whether you want to live all your life with this fellow or that one.

Temptation is another giant you are facing—tempted to lie, to cheat, to fall into lust, and you don't know how to handle these giants. You've been defeated so many times you're like the hound dog that had its tail stepped on so

29

many times that every time he saw someone coming, he just stuck out his tail and waited! You've become the Devil's slave and just say, "Go ahead!" whether it is cheating on an exam, stealing a parked car, disobeying your parents, or not going to church. Satan wins every time because you don't have the power within you to stand up and fight and win.

Now, the secret of killing these giants is seen in David's life. *Here was a young man who had made a decision to serve God.* Way out in the fields, beside some campfire, David had committed his life to God. He didn't know it then, but he was going to become one of the greatest generals in history and one of the greatest kings. He was going to be one of the greatest writers and musicians the world had ever known. And it all started when he was a teenager and he gave his life to God.

The Bible says, "Remember now thy creator in the days of thy youth." Give your life to Christ while you are young and you have all your life ahead of you. The older you get, the harder it will be to make this decision. The years are like the rings in a tree that get harder and harder with the passing of time. The Spirit of God is tugging at your heart asking you to give your life to Christ. Accept His challenge! Christ will change your life, put a sparkle in your eye, a spring in your step, and joy in your soul. Believe me, Jesus Christ will make something out of you!

Then, *David had faith to win battles when he was alone.* God helped him kill a bear that had attacked his sheep. He also killed a lion by trusting God for the strength. That takes a pretty good fellow, but he did it! God helps you win the smaller battles that prepare you for the giants that are ahead.

David also practised his faith in daily life. He did chores around the house. He took family responsibilities seriously and didn't waste time in idleness. When David had time on his hands, he didn't hop in a hot-rod and race down the highway chasing some girl! No! He spent that time with God, wth his harp, learning to praise God. He studied history; he read the Old Testament Scriptures and got to know God. There in the wilderness, all alone, David was being moulded and prepared for leadership. *If you want to be a leader some day, you have to start now!*

And then, *David didn't give up when people sneered at him and rebuked him.* Some of the soldiers said, "You little rascal! Get back to watching your sheep. You talk about killing the giant! Let us take care of that!" But David was willing to stand alone. He let them sneer and call him names: he was ready to stand up for God and he didn't care what happened. Nothing could change him or frighten him and he stood his ground. When you give your life to Jesus Christ there will be some old birds that will come around and say, "Why you sissy—chicken!" You just stand up for Christ and they'll respect you deep down inside, even though they laugh at you.

David didn't fall for their unspiritual advice either. They took David to King Saul, and the king said, "Now look here, you'll have to have some armour to fight that giant, so you can have mine, Get my sword and spear. Don't be a fool, David. Everyone wears armour in a battle!" *Everybody does it!* But not David! You'll be in a classroom some day and some teacher will deny the Bible and say, "Don't swallow that stuff! Nobody believes that any more!" You can't put God in a test tube or a mathematical formula. If you could, He wouldn't be God! No, we accept these things by faith. When I see Jesus hanging on the cross and shedding His blood, I don't understand it all, but I accept it by faith. When you go out to face giants, teenagers, don't depend on your own weapons. Put your faith in Christ, for the Bible says, "Greater is He that is in you than he that is in the world."

There is nothing easy about the Christian life. We have to wrestle with and fight the giants in our lives. Jesus Christ demands your all, and He says that this Christian life is a wrestling match. But He'll give you the supernatural strength to win the battle. David stood before Goliath just a young boy, and said, "I come to thee in the name of the Lord of Hosts, the God of the armies of Israel whom thou hast defied." I am persuaded that in America today we are fighting the wrong war with the wrong weapons on the wrong battlefield in the wrong way. My faith is not in our H-bomb or our armed might. My faith is in God! "For we wrestle not against flesh and blood, but against principalities, against powers, against the rulers of the darkness of this world, against spiritual wickedness in high places." All of us are fighting a spiritual battle, and the Bible commands us to be clothed with the sword of the Spirit, the shield of faith, the helmet of salvation, the breastplate of righteousness, with our feet shod with the preparation of the Gospel of peace. This is the only way to win!

The battle of the ages is going on right now in your heart. You're being pulled in this direction and that, and Satan is battling for your soul with everything he has. Your soul is worth more than the whole world, for Jesus said, "What shall it profit a man if he should gain the whole world and lose his own soul?" You stand in that valley of decision, with the saints and the hosts of heaven on one side and the demons of hell on the other side, and a warfare is raging. The devil says, "Stay with me!" and God says, "Come to the cross and be a Christian soldier!" If you don't take your stand for Christ you will be on the wrong side and some day when it is too late, you'll cry out, "I've taken the wrong stand!" You'll be in the devil's trap!

You can't lick the devil. David didn't go out in his own strength: he went in the power of God! You can defeat these giants only in the power of Christ, the power of the Holy Spirit. David put a stone in his sling—he picked up *five* stones because Goliath had four brothers according to the Bible—and said, "This day will the Lord deliver thee into mine hand!" And David threw the stone, hit Goliath right in the forehead, and the Philistines saw their champion collapse on the battlefield! How did David do it? *In the strength and power of God.*

The only way you can meet the giants in your life— the problems, the situations, the temptations, the sins—is to trust God. You need Jesus Christ as your Saviour. Give your life to Christ and He will wipe your past clean, forgive you of every sin, and give you the power to kill the giants. Receive Him into your life *now*.

BILLY GRAHAM ANSWERS YOUTH'S QUESTIONS

Mr. Graham, do you think that teenagers in foreign countries are more responsive to the Gospel than here in North America?

Teenagers in Europe are just as responsive to the Gospel as they are in North America. There is a great hunger for the Gospel among the youth of Europe. However, there is not as much emphasis upon youth as there is in North America. More teenagers in Europe are working. I also discovered that they are healthier than those in North America. One reason might well be that they do not sit around in front of television sets or spend time in taverns as do so many youth in the United States and Canada.

Mr. Graham, do you believe that too many young people are entering full-time Christian service merely as a convenient way of making a living?

No, not at all. Face it. You can make a better living in many other places than in the ministry or other phases of Christian service. Most Christian workers today are underpaid.

Mr. Graham, what per cent of the people who make decisions in your meetings really mean them and stick to them?

Statistics of one of our recent crusades showed that well over 60 per cent of those who made decisions stuck by them. In other places it is higher. From reading about Jesus in Luke 8 we see that the seed falls in four types of people. Jesus had twelve disciples. One betrayed Him, one denied Him and the rest ran when the going got tough. Some of those who make decisions in our crusades show little growth thereafter.

Mr. Graham, as a leader in a Bible club, I would like to know at what age and where sex education should be taught. Christian education committees are in doubt as to whether it is the job of the church. School systems, under giggles and sneers, teach only briefly the scientific side of the picture. Parents find themselves lost for words and unable to present it well enough to their teenagers.

Basically, sex education is a parental responsibility. If there has been failure along this line it should be placed upon the parents. It is wrong to expect our schools or other institutions to take over a job which is the duty of the parents in the home.

Mr. Graham, do you think that North American teenagers have a greater desire to win their age group to Christ than do youth of Europe? Also, have you noticed any general inconsistency in the lives of North American Christian teenagers.

North American teenagers seem to have a far greater desire to win others to Christ. You must remember, however, that there are thousands more Christian youth in North America than in Europe. European youth who do know Christ have a depth that is missing in the Christian youth of North America. This is especially true in Great Britain, where the knowledge of the Bible among youth is sturdy and solid.

Mr. Graham, how can a young person discern the will of God for his or her life?

This is an important question for all young people today. It would take too much space to answer it here. Let me say this. Get for yourself Bob Cook's book, *It's Tough to Be a Teenager*. It has the answer to your question, written in a wonderful, effective way.

Mr. Graham, do you believe that North American teenagers, as a whole, are spiritual morons?

I'm glad you said North America, for the only recent statistics I have are from Canada. A recent Gallup poll in Canada showed that only one in eight Canadian young people could name six apostles and only a small percentage could name the first book of the Bible. I must say this: there is a vast and appalling ignorance of religious matters all across North America.

Mr. Graham, did the teenagers of England, France, Germany and Sweden come out to hear you in as great numbers as those here in the U.S.A. and Canada?

I would say they came out in just as great numbers in Europe as in North America. There is a great hunger among the youth of the countries you mentioned. It is much easier to reach the youth than it is the adults.

Mr. Graham, much has been written recently about the great "back to God" movement supposedly engulfing America. Do you feel that this will be a lasting revival and what would you say are the main reasons behind its origin?

The reasons for the movement are many : rationalism, failure of materialism, etc. We also must keep three different things in mind: (1) awakening (2) revival (3) evangelistic opportunity. An awakening is not necessarily a revival. I feel that at this present moment we are experiencing a time of unprecedented evangelistic opportunity. There is as yet no sense of the genuine revival for which we long have been praying. God is giving us new avenues of witnessing for Christ and we must go all out to take advantage of them.

Mr. Graham, how would you approach unsaved friends concerning Christ and salvation when the majority of them believe only in their own faiths?

The greatest way to witness is through the life you live. Let the radiance of your Christian life be such that it will make them ask questions about it. Be careful of false piety and the "chip on the shoulder" attitude. Be gracious, sweet and humble. Then let God work through you.

Mr. Graham, what can we as Christian youth do to further the spread of the Gospel in Europe?

35

The main way is to pray. North American youth who go to Europe on their own and without too much experience cannot make too much contribution unless accompanied by older, experienced people. The customs in those countries are totally different than here. Enthusiasm often can give the wrong impression. If you plan to go as a missionary, it is an entirely different question.

Mr. Graham, there has been increasing talk of a spiritual awakening in Britain and on the continent. There also has been more talk recently of a more optimistic world outlook, politically speaking. Do you think these statements are true and are they related?

Yes, I feel the statements are true and there is a tie up between them. There is a relaxation of tension and fear and I believe it is partially due to the prayers of God's people. I do not believe there has been any basic change in Communistic policy. They realise that the only alternative to peace is a war of annihilation. There is unparalleled spiritual hunger in Europe today.

Mr. Graham, from the standpoint of the high schooler, do we have much to look forward to in life? Is the world going to pot? Or is it turning back to God? People say that church attendance is increasing, but so is juvenile delinquency. If the world keeps on getting worse, we youth of today do not have a bright future, do we?

Because you have seen so much of the world and its conditions, would you say we have a brighter tomorrow coming? Or are people rebelling against God all the more?

For the Christian, the world is never going to pot. No matter what the circumstances, we have Christ. Of course, no one can foresee the future. Our great hope is the second coming of Christ and we live with that glorious anticipation.

It is doubtful if young people today can plan to live as normal a life as did their parents. The hydrogen bomb threat and shadow is the only thing that keeps the world from blowing itself apart, and we never know when some madman will push the button.

But let me repeat. We as Christians have the wonderful hope of the second coming of Christ and being with Him no matter what happens.

Mr. Graham, in discussing the various phases of your ministry with friends, a question has arisen. about what per cent of the people who see your films accept Christ as their personal Saviour in comparison to those who accept Christ when they hear you in person? And, if you find that more people accept Christ through viewing the films, would you not have greater results if more time was given to the film ministry?

Among those who view our films, about the same percentage come forward to receive Christ per capita as in our crusades. I think it is possible that we might see greater results, but I am spreading too thin now so that I cannot give any more time to it.

BILLY GRAHAM ON MISSIONS

▶The supreme task of the church is not revival, but to preach the Gospel to every creature. Whether their skin be black or yellow, red or white, it's our job to reach them with the Gospel.

▶God gave us but one great command, "Go ye into all the world and preach the Gospel." Soldiers in an army would be court-martialled if they treated their officers' orders in the cavalier fashion with which we have treated this Great Commission.

▶God never calls a man without equipping him. I know that from experience. I fought God when He called me to preach, but I'll never forget the joy and thrill that came to my soul when God said to me, "Billy, I'll take what you've got and use you."

▶The motto I have taken for my life is "To evangelise the world in this generation, that every person might hear the Gospel once before the others have heard it twice."

▶We see in Ezekiel 3 that God says, in effect, "I'll hold you responsible to witness to the heathen and to the wicked. If the wicked and heathen turn not from his heathenish and wicked way, then will I not require their blood from your hand. But IF YOU FAIL to carry the Gospel of Jesus Christ to the wicked and the heathen, THEIR BLOOD WILL BE ON YOUR HANDS."

▶To date, after fifty generations, only 35 per cent of the people on the earth have heard the Gospel presented. Many of us have aimed the wrong way. I know of one church which spent more than $500,000 in a building programme in four years. During the same time it spent only $15,000 for foreign missions.

▶What is your answer as we look on the whitened harvest fields? If He is Lord, there is but one answer we can honestly make, "Here am I, Lord, send me, take me, use me as Thou shalt choose." Will you make it?